How NOT to Get Ripped Off as an Heir

Contents

ı

Introduction

Did you know that your role as a beneficiary or heir is just as important as that of the executor/executrix and that you usually don't find out until a loved one has passed and an executor or executrix has been appointed. And even more important, did you know that since there is no one to police the estate, that things can go wrong and you can lose out on assets and/or money to which you are entitled?

The problem is that no one really says anything, especially an executor, who feels that he or she is privy to everything and that beneficiaries are not privy to anything,, unless he or she says so.

How would you know this? And what would you miss by not knowing?

Plenty.

This ebook has been written as a basic guide for beneficiaries. Chapter 1, for example, fills you in on beneficiaries' rights, among them the right to call out an unscrupulous executor.

In Chapter 2, you learn why beneficiaries should be involved and work as a team. Chapter 3 outlines some common problems that may happen at the beginning of probate, while Chapter 4 briefly explains the executor's role and how it is abused. Chapter 5 gives you the basics of complaining and Chapter 6 includes ideas for selecting and hiring the best estate lawyer for your estate issues. And finally, Chapter 7 gives you the low-down on why it is so crucial to review the estate's final accounting.

Having learned important lessons from the probate of my aunt's estate and the antics of an unscrupulous executrix and her CPA, I thought it was unfair for future beneficiaries and heirs to put up with tactics and tricks that shortchange them out of what they are rightfully entitled to. I've been there and done that --- playing phone tag, dealing with people who regard an estate's affairs as military secrets and simply refuse to share much information or help to expedite matters.

1.   Beneficiaries Have Rights Too

For the longest time, I believed that someone else, such as the executor, would be honest, forthright and communicative. That person would handle the nuts-and-bolts of an estate competently, allowing me and other beneficiaries time for other things like grieving the decedent. And whatever took place was normal and was :supposed" to happen.

But things don't always happen the way in which they are supposed to. The decedent's wishes aren't always respected or handled correctly. And the beneficiaries are the last to know.

By the time they find out, it is too late.

However, as a beneficiary, you are not supposed to allow people as executors, estate lawyers and accountants boss you around or run amok with an estate's assets and in particular, the assets that were set aside for you. This leads to the first right:

. Beneficiaries have the right to know what is happening with a loved one's estate..

And the people, such as executors, who are in charge of administering the estate, are responsible for informing beneficiaries from time to time. Usually, the estate lawyer sends a letter to each beneficiary that details necessary information in a timely manner. But the executor is equally responsible and make the time to notify beneficiaries of what he or she has done so far and planning to do.

.Beneficiaries have the right to "fire" an executor who mismanages an estate, either on purpose or through ignorance. The

executor isn't an independent entity in any sense of the word.

Typically, beneficiaries (as a group) should consider filing a complaint with the probate court early on in the administration of an estate. In most cases, they can hire a competent probate attorney to help them do this. Such an attorney will have to be paid. If the beneficiaries agree to share a necessary expense, such as this one, they will likely be successful.

. Beneficiaries have the right to insist that an executor be bonded before administering an estate, especially if there are any doubts about an executor's honesty or scruples.

A bond is similar to that of insurance in that an executor could be required to pay back stolen money and other valuables. Of course, a bond isn't always featured in an estate because it is an added expense for the estate.

. Beneficiaries have the right to insist that the court appoint someone to accompany an executor. If an executor is believed to be dishonest and likely be tempted to remove estate assets for his or her own use, with no intentions of informing beneficiaries, that is considered illegal.

This is a very effective option because it frees up beneficiaries' time while keeping an executor honest. A probate court is more likely to believe a person whom they designate for the task.

Important fact: No one is available to "police" an estate, making it imperative for those who have a stake in its assets receive what is rightfully theirs.

. Beneficiaries have a right to a final estate accounting, which they should scrutinize for inaccuracies or exaggerations or omitted items and have a say in expressing concerns.

An unscrupulous executor or CPA could hold up distribution of this document for months and years, hoping that the whole matter will go away. This will not happen if beneficiaries are enlightened, alert and aware. If a CPA has shortchanged the estate, his or her mistakes or omissions will become obvious immediately. Of course, an unscrupulous CPA who fears getting into trouble will avoid submitting such a document altogether, hoping that beneficiaries will remain naïve and ignorant.

As stated earlier, **no one polices an estate. Making sure that everything is done properly is really the beneficiaries' responsibility.**

2.   With Teamwork, Results are Possible

With no one to police and protect estates, the burden, not surprisingly, falls on beneficiaries. The voice of a lone beneficiary will not be taken seriously as several beneficiaries Beneficiaries working as a team and maintaining contact with the executor and estate lawyer, show that they are a force to be reckoned with, especially when discrepancies appear or problems with an executor occur. There's strength in numbers.

This is why it is imperative for beneficiaries coordinate their plans and efforts as a team right from the onset. Everyone involved needs to realize that being passive and allowing the executor, estate lawyer and even the accountants full control of an estate. Who knows what these professionals' agendas really are? And who knows if these people are truly honest and do what they promise to do? Beneficiaries cannot and should never assume that an estate will be handled well. Instead, they need to avoid being passive and become involved.

Beneficiaries acting as a united front convey an important message to an executor, namely, that nonsense and dishonesty will not be tolerated.

Knowing that he or she is under scrutiny, and risks problems if he or she attempts to take advantage at any point, an executor may think twice before stealing from the estate and shortchanging its beneficiaries. After all, he knows that his efforts will be under watchful eyes until the estate is closed.

Beneficiaries support each other and act as a sounding board for one another.

Not one beneficiary is left out of the loop. Every beneficiary knows that he or she can, with the others, opt to hire an estate lawyer, or not. If two beneficiaries are children of deceased parents, they have the right to enter their home and remove their parents' items without an executor's permission.

Beneficiaries, acting as a team, can confront an executor and have him or her removed.

An executor or executrix is not a king or queen, but another human being who isn't perfect and can steal or mismanage an estate. The task of collecting and assembling documents in proving allegations can be delegated to two or more beneficiaries who have some time and desire to help.

3.   Problems Must Be Addressed ASAP

As estate probate continues, beneficiaries must not allow themselves to be lulled into a sense of false security. They need to stay on top of things with updates from the executor.

This means visiting the probate court in person once the will has been filed, you as a beneficiary may view the file to see what the executor has been up to so far and obtain copies of desired files.

No one, aside from your estate attorney, will inform you of this. Possibly, that professional views this as a matter that he or she can handle for you, thus having an excuse to charge you for a service that you don't need.

In any case, you should consider visiting the court after two or three weeks have passed and reviewing/obtaining copies of desired files. You may be surprised at what you find, such as the executor being paid a double fee for a service that's already been paid. You may also discover that another CPA has been hired. You may notice expenses that don't seem relevant to the estate, yet are charged to the estate.

To be sure, each beneficiary should review documents, jot down questions and concerns, which should be forwarded to the probate court.

 Be aware, also, of red flags, such as weeks and even months that pass with no word from a dishonest, secretive estate lawyer or executor. Before long, a substantial amount of time will have been lost, along with great results, because beneficiaries did not contact the estate lawyer or executor for updates.

To a disreputable estate attorney, executor and CPAs, loss of so much time is not a big deal (for them), but is and should be a big concern for beneficiaries. In fact, beneficiaries need to report the executor or executrix to the probate court and possibly have that person removed and replaced. Lengthy silence should not be tolerated, but investigated, especially if one or two beneficiaries have bought up concerns to an executor and are still waiting for an answer.

Waiting a long time for a response from the executor If after a two or three-week waiting period for a report passes, with no word from the executor and/or estate lawyer, something is clearly wrong and should be dealt with immediately. . This problem may be due to mismanagement of the estate on the part of the executor and/or estate lawyer. Other factors include dishonest, undisclosed acts, such as theft and excuses.

In one case, for example, a frustrated estate lawyer complained that the executor and her CPAs were "running the show." That is, he wasn't getting information/updates from the professionals involved, who apparently chose not to share information with him, nor did either show any signs of doing so.

To deal with this problem, beneficiaries need to contact the executor by phone or e-mail, letting him or her know their concerns and requesting a report on what has been going on. If no response is forthcoming in a reasonable time, beneficiaries need to make repeated contacts until someone can provide answers.

Waiting too long will only cause this potential problem to fester and even grow over time. In addition to repeated contacts, beneficiaries need to begin and maintain a written journal containing dates and notes. Who was spoken to and when? What response was given? What happened after that?

The executor chastises or threatens beneficiaries
Make a note of this immediately! What did he or she say and when? Were any other responses given?

In addition, it's never a good idea to dismiss this event. Someone, preferably one or more of the beneficiaries, need respond immediately. They should consider hiring a good estate lawyer and having that lawyer help them submit a complaint against the executor to the probate court. Beneficiaries should also share the expense of retaining a good estate lawyer. More on this later.

Items disappear from the estate/decedent's home

Evidently, the decedent's home remained unprotected from any outside intruders, such as a burglar or even an unbounded executor himself! These incidents must be noted and reported immediately. And if possible, a list of missing items should be made and provided to police and other authorities.

4. The Executor is *Not* the Beneficiaries' Boss

A well-chosen executor, though a family member, will handle the onerous chore of administering an estate competently. But sadly, that relative will also be in a perfect position to commit fraud, with power and complete access to a decedent's home and other assets.

That relative may have other issues going on as well, such as having a sense of entitlement, along the lines of "I made sure that the decedent got everything she needed and wanted when he or she was alive, so I deserve a reward" etc., etc. Or that relative may still be secretly holding grievances or grudges against certain beneficiaries and feels a need to "get even" by withholding certain assets, like money, and updates on what he or she, the executor, removed from the estate. In his or her mind, ignorant, unsophisticated beneficiaries deserve what they get.

So overall, a corrupt executor can easily take advantage of the situation and beneficiaries, overlooking that his or her key duty is that of serving others, not primarily himself or herself. And to add injury to insult, get away with it.

However, this problem can and should be anticipated and even eliminated if beneficiaries as a team insist that an executor or executrix must be bonded. If he or she commits a dishonest act, such as stealing, he or she can be made to repay the stolen amount of money. But unless someone does raise questions and say something, a dishonest executor can wait until the estate is closed, and be "home free."

Yet even after probate has begun, observant beneficiaries can keep a record of the fraud committed and obtain relief. They can note dates and items as missed calls, deadlines and reports. They can record excuses verbatim from the executrix. And at some later point, beneficiaries can retain an estate attorney to help sort matters out. The sooner they act in this regard, the better.

Four signs of a corrupt executor/executrix

. An executor openly makes it clear that he or she has the last word and uses this attitude to take advantage of others, such as beneficiaries.

. The executor rarely communicates with beneficiaries. When pressed for an answer, an executor will remain silent for as long as possible or at the very least, provide a short one, if at all.

. The executor tries to prohibit decedents' children from entering their parents' property and retrieving decedents' personal items. It is a good idea to find out if this is true in your state as well.

. Takes longer than a few weeks or even months before communicating. He or she tends to show similar regard for the estate lawyer. In one case, an estate lawyer expressed his frustration for being kept waiting, saying, "They're running the show!"

. Sets up artificial barriers to efforts in settling an estate. An executor, for example, instructed the estate lawyer to prepare and issue a release to be signed as a condition for gaining access to funds that one beneficiary was entitled to. The release consisted of as many as four pages. And although the release was signed and notarized in a timely manner, it was ultimately disregarded by an executrix and the estate lawyer. Instead, the executrix stated that she herself would not sign the release, thus holding back progress in efforts to resolve the situation.

How beneficiaries can deal with a corrupt executor

. Understand the meaning of "probate fraud," which is an executor's attempt to deprive beneficiaries' rightful share of the estate's assets. Not all states apply the same laws and regulations for dealing with probate fraud, so beneficiaries can easily find out by googling the name of their state before or after the words, "probate fraud." Armed with that information, beneficiaries will be able to apply their knowledge to the situation.

Have the probate court exercise supervision over the executor's actions, but find out if this is possible in your state. If so, you might want to consider retaining an estate lawyer, who can also let you know what your rights are.

. If you and the other beneficiaries think that an executor is committing fraud, you'll need evidence, such as letters, notices, accounting reports, to have him or her removed from his or her position early on in the probate process. Written accounts, aka journals that you have kept which indicate an executor's pattern of behavior and fraud. You should, of course, consult with an estate attorney for his or her opinion on the matter and help in filing a claim against the executor. Also consider challenging the executor in probate court. It is a good idea to consult your estate attorney for the procedure.

. Sometimes you and the other beneficiaries can force a corrupt executor to reveal his or her hand. Let's say, for example, that the executor wants you to sign a release of some sort, knowing that once you do, you will not be able to file any claims or make the executor accountable. You just may be able to demand something else as a condition for your signature --- and have the executor agree. For example, you may want (and are entitled to) a copy of the last accounting. So you hold off on signing anything until you receive that document!

Caveat: A corrupt executor is not likely to agree, knowing that once the final accounting document is in your hands, you can, will and should scrutinize it for inconsistencies and exaggerations --- and complain about them.

Maybe one complaint from a single beneficiary may not matter, but complaints from *all* of the beneficiaries *do matter!* Those complaints will definitely attract attention and possibly bring about desired results.

5 Does Complaining Help?

It depends.

At the very least, it draws attention to a problem and the culprits who caused it. Beneficiaries are able to vent and line up support. At its worst, complaining doesn't produce results, such as causing a CPA to lose his or her license.

As a beneficiary, I would definitely be aware of what is going, during probate, especially if the executor was unbonded. What tends to happen is that one problem doesn't stand alone. It could be related to an earlier problem that was unobserved and whose presence is becoming more obvious. Something needs to be done about it, as it is going to keep festering.

So bringing attention to that problem could help in that someone else knows about it. But the real question to be answered is, will that someone do something about it, like bringing the guilty party, such as CPAs, to task?

Not really. Typically when a complaint arrives, it's not handled right away, simply because such a board has to deal with so many complaints at one time. In the meantime, your complaint is languishing in a big pile of papers in someone's inbox for God knows how long. Yours will receive needed attention when its time is due and not a minute less.

So you wind up waiting and waiting and waiting.

Then the board will likely "investigate" the matter by contacting the guilty party and notifying it of your complaint. After a certain number of weeks and/or months, the board will contact you via postal mail and letting you know the results.

In most cases, the results will be disappointing. Based on the information you provided in your complaint, such a board will state that the information was "insufficient" and the case is now closed.

How can that be?

Typically, such examiners' boards get large numbers of correspondence from outside sources. As you might expect, the majority of this correspondence concerns a complaint about someone. Given large numbers of these complaints, the board picks and chooses ones deemed worthy of further investigation. Or not.

Complaining to the BBB

In a book on complaining effectively, an author stated that if a state board of examiners couldn't or wouldn't do anything to help you, you should contact your state's Better Business Bureau (BBB).

Implementing that advice sounds like a good idea and it is, if you happen to be complaining about a landscaper or other business. If that's the case, you can feel confident that the BBB will deal effectively with the complaint and possibly get desired results as refunds, for example.

You won't. What you will get is a letter stating that no problem was found and the case is closed, unless you wish to respond within 10 days. Your explanation will likely fall on deaf ears and before long, a formal written letter will be on its way to you, stating that the case is closed now and forever.

But trust me, you're not the only one this has happened to. All you have to do is google "complaints about the BBB" and you'll find numerous entries.

If you are able to reach a contact, such as the estate lawyer, by phone, do the following:

. Plan ahead. That means writing down the first thing you want to say to the lawyer. Make a list of points that you want to bring up during your discussion. And have them on paper right in front of you when the lawyer answers the phone. For example, you can begin by saying, "I'm --------------- ----------------- , calling in regard to the ----------------- ----------estate, and have a question."

. *Don't fall for "He'll call you back."*Right. Like that's going to happen. You'll wind up spending a whole day waiting for a call that you'll never get. Follow up immediately instead. If a lawyer's secretary says, "He'll call you back," get to the nitty-gritty by insisting on a time frame, say 1pm to 3 pm. Or better yet, let her know by saying that you'll call back at such and such a time. Doing that implies that you are in control. You shouldn't have to be at other people's beck and call, especially in matters involving an estate. The time you lose could easily be your own.

. Contact the other beneficiaries, let them know what's happening and encourage them to contact an elusive executor or estate lawyer.

Doing those things should get the ball rolling.

Another way to complain is to contact government agencies, such as state examiner boards. They are further removed from executors and lawyers and their interests. And their memberships are comprised of professionals, such as attorneys or accountants. Often, these agencies' websites feature complaint forms that allow you to complain directly online.

It's always a good idea to visit those websites and review the complaint forms. You'll have a better idea of specific details you'll need to provide, such as names, dates, and incidents. You'll also find out if additional forms or documents are needed. So the word to the wise is become familiar with unknown territory first. Then plunge in as soon as you're ready.

Prepare further by finding out exactly what a given agency is seeking in a complaint. Not knowing what is being sought can cost you a lot of time and hours of effort. You could always contact the agency directly and ask point-blank. Get names, phone numbers and/or emails. You'll never know when this information will come in handy someday.

Sometimes in answering your question, an agency representative may honestly admit that, like an art lover, they'll recognize a compellingly-written complaint when they see it. Don't buy it! Instead, do some sleuthing and start googling. You may begin by typing in the name of the agency or asking a question relating to your complaint and see what comes up. Chances are that you'll be surprised --- and in some cases, shocked. In some cases, you will want to keep your expectations low.

6. Should You Hire an Estate Attorney?

The answer is usually yes. An estate attorney can obtain answers and get access to documents and professionals more easily than an individual beneficiary ever could. I found that out after playing phone tag for nearly three months simply because I thought I was *saving money and a hassle. A few more weeks passed before I finally* contacted an attorney who specialized in estates and had more than twenty years' of experience in dealing with all aspects of them.

So beneficiaries might want to invest money in such an attorney, saving time and getting results sooner than if they each worked independently.

When an attorney may be needed

Even though an attorney need not be hired right away, it is to beneficiaries' advantage to know which attorney they can depend upon and call should the need arise. Issues involving estate attorneys and executors or with extended families can come up at any time when they are least expected. Instead of wasting time figuring out what to do and when on their own, beneficiaries owe it to themselves to contact and possibly retain an attorney. Sure, fees have to be paid, but normally, those fees are less expensive than the amount of money in an estate.

Finding and Hiring an Attorney

An attorney who can serve you and beneficiaries the best isn't easy to find. Beneficiaries may begin by asking family members and friends for likely attorneys. But the search shouldn't be limited to family and friends. It can be extended to lawyers who are already known. Contact your state's Bar Association for more recommendations. Then contact and interview each attorney over the phone. Have a list of questions on a notepad nearby and a pen handy.

Questions to Ask a Prospective Estate Attorney

. How much experience have you had in handling estates?

. Have you ever dealt with dishonest, uncooperative executors?

. How much do you charge per hour?

. Do you provide your clients with a list of itemized expenses per billing period?

7 Obtain and Review an Estate's Final Accounting

Receiving and carefully reviewing the estate's final accounting is crucial for all beneficiaries! And the executor or executrix *must provide* this to beneficiaries. If an executor or executrix fails to do this for any reason, beneficiaries can be assured that there's a problem.

Why an executor or executrix may not provide a final accounting to beneficiaries

Basically, an executor lacks integrity and honesty in that he or she has something to hide. That something may be include insufficient documentation, such as receipts and timesheets of expenses to the estate. That document could also include a number of errors made by an accountant.

In my own case, the executrix and her CPAs emphatically told my estate attorney that they had no intentions of answering his questions. What happened was that he scrutinized a draft and found unaccounted=for items as an extra payment to the executrix, minus explanations/documentation as timesheets. He also found that the executrix skimmed money off the beneficiaries' inheritance tax payments without cause.

Another reason is that an executor or executrix wants to avoid paying taxes on the money, while indicating at the same time that beneficiaries are liable for all taxes due from their inheritances.

. And finally, the executor or executrix fears that he or she will be prosecuted, based on his or her dishonesty.

So what can beneficiaries do to avoid problems?

Beneficiaries should not sign anything until a final accounting is provided. If beneficiaries sign any "releases" or similar documents in advance, they relinquish their rights for good, as the estate is closed. And even worse, the executor gets away with everything, including assets and/or money that beneficiaries were entitled to and should have received.

Beneficiaries, as a group, should make it very clear that the final accounting is provided and not sign *anything* until that documentation is provided.